Long Live Life

Cover and interior design by Maulik Mehta.

ISBN - 978-9356554245

Published by - Swati Joshi

First Edition: 2026

For inquiries, contact: stories@swatisjournal.com

A GENTLE PHILOSOPHY FOR MEANING, HAPPINESS, AND HUMAN CONNECTION

Long Live Life

SWATI JOSHI

Dedication

To those quietly choosing meaning over noise.
To the ones who still believe gentleness can make a difference.
This is for you.

Preface

Welcome to **Long Live Life**, a gentle guide to living with purpose, joy, connection, and legacy. Over the next twenty chapters, we'll explore foundational values, mind mastery, social richness, and soulful vision.

Before we begin, I'd like to introduce a simple but powerful framework you'll find woven throughout this book, the **LIFE Method**. It's not a rigid system, but a set of compass points to help you navigate each section with intention.

- **Listen**: Cultivate the art of tuning into your inner voice and truly hearing others. This is the root of empathy and self-awareness.
- **Integrate**: Move beyond insight to action. Turn philosophical ideas into small, daily rituals that shape your character and habits.

- **Flow:** Embrace life's natural rhythms, knowing when to wait, when to act, and when to rest. Flow is the balance between doing and being.
- **Evolve:** Reflect on your journey and contribute to something larger than yourself. Evolving means growing personally and leaving a legacy of goodness.

You'll see reminders of **Listen**, **Integrate**, **Flow**, and **Evolve** at meaningful moments, but don't worry about checking every box. The goal is to guide, not to overwhelm.

Carry this framework in your mind as you read. Test it, adapt it, and make it your own. Let the 'LIFE Method' be a companion as you explore these pages and, ultimately, your own life.

Here's to the journey ahead, may it deepen your understanding, enrich your days, and help you live your life well!

Swati Joshi

About the Author

Swati Joshi has spent her life listening.

As a paramedic, she witnessed human fragility and resilience in moments of crisis. As an educator, she watched how people learn, grow, and sometimes stumble. As a writer, she translates these observations into wisdom that actually matters.

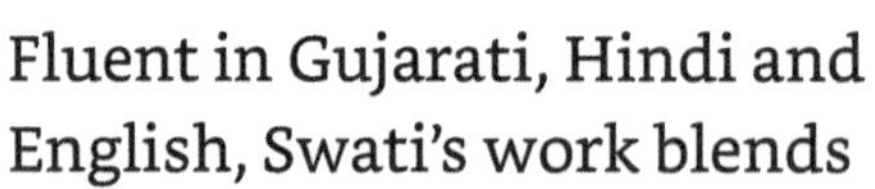

Fluent in Gujarati, Hindi and English, Swati's work blends

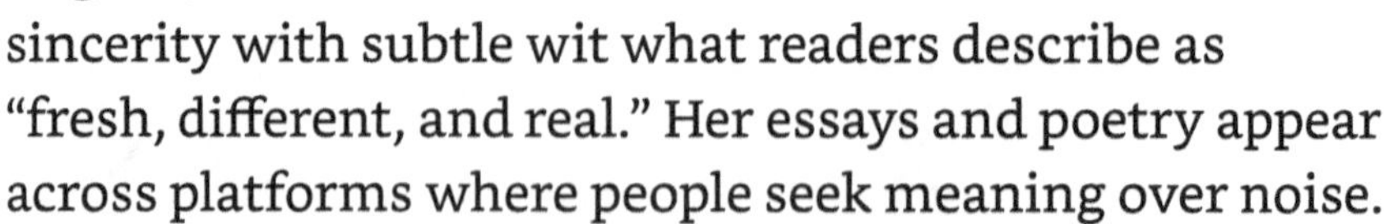

sincerity with subtle wit what readers describe as "fresh, different, and real." Her essays and poetry appear across platforms where people seek meaning over noise.

She holds a background in science and paramedical fields, and has devoted years to teaching and community work. But her true education comes from relationships, family dinners, difficult conversations and moments of quiet grace.

Long Live Life is the philosophy she built from these experiences, not for the perfectly ambitious people, but for the quietly intentional ones.

Connect with Swati:

Visit swatisjournal.com for essays and reflections, or reach out at stories@swatisjournal.com

Table of Content

PART 1

Foundations Of A Meaningful Life

Discover the core values that give life its soul.

This section explores the internal groundwork needed to live a joyful, intentional life. Through stories of humility, belief, acceptance, and emotional self-awareness, these chapters build the psychological roots of the 'LIFE Method'.

Readers are invited to reflect on their mindset, habits, and self-talk while taking gentle steps toward presence and peace.

1. A Little Help Would Help
2. Keep The Faith
3. Listen Within
4. The Gift Of Acceptance
5. The Blessing Of Gratitude

1

CHAPTER I

A Little Help Would Help

CHAPTER 1: A LITTLE HELP WOULD HELP

A few years ago, I found myself standing in line at a hospital, juggling a sick child, paperwork, and the silent panic of uncertainty. A stranger behind me, without a word, held my place in line while I stepped aside to soothe my child. She didn't offer advice. She didn't fix anything. She simply showed up in that small, human way.

It was then I realized that help doesn't always arrive with grand gestures. Sometimes, it arrives in silence, in presence!

We often underestimate just how powerful simple acts of support can be. We mostly imagine help to be heroic. But in reality, it's the everyday kindnesses, the ones that go unnoticed, making life more livable.

How much have you lived till now? If counting the years and days passing by is called living, then many of us have lived more than we needed to.

> **Help one another; there's no time like the present and no present like the time. —James Durst**

The world has always longed for immortality. Behind every discovery and invention lies a desire to survive longer or even forever. But in recent times, we've added something more to that longing i.e. happiness.

Now, we aren't just chasing long life, we also want it to be joyful. Yet, life remains a relative term. We constantly compare, measure, and analyze. Our reference points are others, not ourselves. And in this endless race to win, many of us lose peace.

But there's another way. I believe observation is more powerful than analysis. Observing others, their habits, their reactions, their way of life, not with envy, but with openness can teach us how to live better. And watching ourselves in that light can bring perspective.

We can learn, adapt, and perhaps most importantly, help.

Helping others even in small, non-material ways improves our own quality of life. Being present! Listening! Supporting! These count far more than we realize. A kind word, a moment of attention, or even a smile can be help enough.

We don't always have to give money or gifts. Sometimes,

being there is the greatest gift.

And we're allowed to ask for help, too. This give and take knits the fabric of relationships and adds warmth to our days.

In doing so, we may just add years to our lives.

• WHAT LIFE TAUGHT ME •

I still remember the day I nearly talked myself out of asking for help. I had been struggling with a project for weeks, but cockiness and fear kept me silent. One evening, exhausted and out of options, I hesitantly reached out to a friend. What followed was not just support, but an unexpected bond that lifted me beyond the problem itself.

We often treat independence like a badge of honor. We hesitate to ask, to lean, to receive. But life is not meant to be walked alone. The simple act of asking for help can transform not only your situation, but your spirit.

Asking doesn't make you weak. It makes you human.

Sometimes we just need someone to simply be there. Not to fix anything, but to let us feel supported and seen.
— Swati Joshi

> **No one who achieves success does so without the help of others. The wise and confident acknowledge this help with gratitude. — Alfred North Whitehead**

To receive help well:

- Be honest with your need
- Ask clearly and kindly
- Accept support without guilt
- Offer help in return whenever you CAN!

Help given is kindness. Help received is humility. And both are beautiful.

We are mirrors to each other's strengths and soft places to land in each other's struggles. Asking for help invites connection. Offering help builds meaning.

· LET THIS SETTLE WITHIN YOU ·

When was the last time you genuinely asked for help? What stopped you then, and what did you learn from it?

· TRY THIS IN YOUR OWN LIFE ·

Make a list of three areas where you're currently struggling. Next to each one, write down one person who might be able to support you. Reach out to at least one of them this week, not with apology, but with openness.

And what if someone asks you for help? Give with joy. Because when help flows freely, so does life.

Start by hearing yourself: where are you feeling overwhelmed?

• LIFE ECHO: *LISTEN* •

Listening honestly is the first act of courage.

> “A tiny thread of help is strong enough for putting together a tearing life. — Swati Joshi”

2

CHAPTER 2

Keep The Faith

CHAPTER 2: KEEP THE FAITH

Believing in something gives you a kind of inner strength. You believe in good, you become better. And as I've said earlier, acceptance follows belief indiscriminately.

We live in a world where training programs promise personal transformation overnight. But real change doesn't come from a crash course. It comes from years of conscious effort, repeated actions in a consistent direction. Life is chaotic, unpredictable. Belief and

> **Faith is the patience of a seed waiting under the dark earth for the spring it hasn't seen yet. - Swati Joshi**

acceptance are the oars we use to row through its tides.

Humans think and plan, and with that comes the tendency to blame ourselves for everything that goes wrong. But consider this, animals, trees, rivers all live without such guilt, without overthinking. They believe in nature and simply respond to it.

So what should we believe in?

First and foremost, believe in yourself! You're here not just to survive, but to create memories, to build a legacy, and to inspire those who come after you. You'll become an example worth remembering through not what you preach, but through how you live.

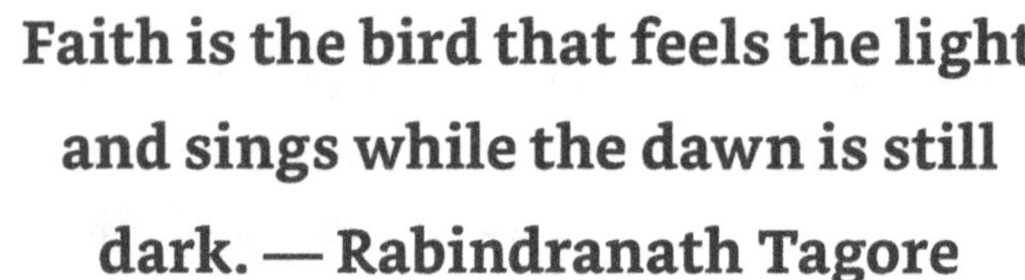

> **Faith is the bird that feels the light and sings while the dawn is still dark. — Rabindranath Tagore**

Also, temper your belief in your own powers. Yes, we're capable of amazing things, but we're not invincible. Setbacks, grief, and adversities are part of life's truth. Faith doesn't mean ignoring them; it means holding on through those tough times.

And above all, trust that **life heals**. Storms come, but they also pass. Not all days are bright. Accepting that helps us prepare and endure. We must believe not only in our strength, but also in our vulnerability.

Belief is not a solitary pursuit. Trusting others is vital. Doubt dominates our modern mindset, but the world runs on trust. Allow people to prove they're worth believing in. And if someone breaks your trust, believe in your own ability to recover.

Keeping the faith is not about staying naïve. It's about staying open.

When you believe in yourself, in others, and in life itself you don't just survive; you grow, and you help others grow too.

> **"To one who has faith, no explanation is necessary. To one without faith, no explanation is possible. — Thomas Aquinas"**

· WHAT LIFE TAUGHT ME ·

There was a time when uncertainty covered my mind. I was dubious about the plan, the path, the point of everything. I'd go to sleep unresolved and wake up even more so. But one morning, without any fuss, I got up and followed the plan anyway. Not because I was sure it would work, just because it seemed worth believing in.

Faith is not blind obedience. It's a quiet decision to trust the process, even when it's unclear.

Belief fuels resilience. It makes space for possibility when logic says, "Give up."

Keeping the faith doesn't mean ignoring doubt. It means choosing hope anyway.

· LET THIS SETTLE WITHIN YOU ·

What do you continue to believe in even when it feels foolish to do so? What holds that belief steady?

· LIFE ECHO: *INTEGRATE* ·

Let your faith shape small, daily choices. Let it show up in your routines and how you treat others.

> **"Faith is like the sea breeze; you set the sails, it keeps you moving forward. — Swati Joshi"**

3

CHAPTER 3

Listen Within

CHAPTER 3: LISTEN WITHIN

Allowing yourself to make mistakes, to take risks, or to choose a path others don't approve of, is a part of what makes you human. It doesn't make you weak; it makes you real.

We often reserve the word "allow" for what we let others do. But what if we turned that inward? What if we allowed ourselves to feel, to fall, to pause or to be imperfect?

In today's hyperconnected world, comparison is an unsolicited and effortless act. A quick scroll can leave us questioning our path. But no two people are raised the same, carry the same scars, or dream in the same colors.

> **Your visions will become clear only when you can look into your own heart. — Carl Jung**

So how could we possibly walk the same road?

Purpose isn't a universal destination. It's a deeply personal journey. And to find it, we must listen, not to noise, but to the silence inside us. That silence, though often uncomfortable, carries answers we won't hear from others.

> **To be vulnerable is to be brave. To listen is to lead. — Brené Brown**

Your inner voice doesn't shout. It waits. And you must learn the art of stillness to hear it.

Facing life's hard truths like its inevitable pains and disappointments is not weakness. Turning toward those truths allows us to receive their hidden teachings. Even anguish has its wisdom.

You will be hurt. You might be misled. But let that not close your heart. Instead, allow yourself to trust again, even knowing the risk. This kind of strength can't be taught it comes through living it.

There's courage in permitting yourself to hope, to care, to forgive, to try again. When you let go the need of always being right, always be in control, it brings you peace.

So allow!

Allow joy.

Allow fear.

Allow mistakes.

Allow healing.

Above all, allow yourself to be exactly who you are becoming.

• WHAT LIFE TAUGHT ME •

When was the last time you sat still long enough to hear yourself think, really think? Not the voice of fear or to-do lists, but the quiet, knowing one that rarely interrupts.

We seek answers outside: in books, experts, algorithms. But often, the wisdom we need is already within us.

Listening within is a skill, a practice, and often a source of deep peace.

Your inner voice may be soft, but it never lies. When you get better at listening, decisions become clearer, and self-respect grows.

• LET THIS SETTLE WITHIN YOU •

What might your inner voice be trying to tell you that you've been avoiding?

• LIFE ECHO: *LISTEN* •

Find quiet moments this week to check in with yourself. Your intuition is not just valid, it's indispensable.

> **That steady voice of 'knowing it', though loud or hushed, is the compass you use while navigating through life. — Swati Joshi**

24

CHAPTER 4

The Gift Of Acceptance

CHAPTER 4: THE GIFT OF ACCEPTANCE

We often confuse acceptance with resignation. But acceptance isn't giving up, it's letting go of what's beyond control, so you can embrace what's within it.

Life, by nature, is imperfect. People will fail you. Plans will derail. Emotions will rise uninvited. When we fight these truths, we suffer twice: once from the event, and again from our resistance to it.

Acceptance is a quiet power. It doesn't demand applause. It simply allows you to breathe deeper, react less, and live more.

Many of us spend years trying to fix what isn't our responsibility to fix; other people's choices, the past, outcomes we can't change. Acceptance says, "This is how it is. Now, what can I do with it?"

Happiness can exist only in acceptance. — George Orwell

It helps us conserve energy for where it matters — our actions, attitudes, and presence.

Practicing acceptance doesn't mean lowering your standards. It means recognizing the difference between effort and outcome. It means letting go of control, not commitment.

> **Acceptance is not submission; it is acknowledgment of the facts of a situation, then deciding what you're going to do about it. — Kathleen Casey Theisen**

When we accept ourselves, with all our flaws, fears, and histories, we stop requiring perfection to feel peace. And when we accept others, even when we disagree, we build bridges that judgment can't.

Acceptance is a gift we give to life, and it gives us clarity in return.

• WHAT LIFE TAUGHT ME •

My daughter keeps stating, "You don't fight enough to fix things in your life!" I tell her that "I've seen my life changing from the day I stopped arguing with reality." At first, she didn't get it. Why not fight to fix things?

I've learnt the truth that some things don't need fixing. They need witnessing.

Acceptance is not surrender. It's alignment.

It's how we stop draining our energy in resistance and start living in peace.

To accept doesn't mean to agree. It means to see clearly, without needing to control.

Acceptance gives us the freedom to grow where we are, not where we wish we were.

· LET THIS SETTLE WITHIN YOU ·

What part of your life are you still resisting? What might happen if you chose to accept it, just as it is, for now?

· LIFE ECHO: *FLOW* ·

Not everything needs your fight. Some things need your softening.

When I let go of what I am, I become what I might be. — Lao Tzu

“To heal the wound, we don’t mourn the mark it has left, instead we check how deep it has cut. — Swati Joshi”

CHAPTER 5

The Blessing Of Gratitude

CHAPTER 5: THE BLESSING OF GRATITUDE

In our constant pursuit of more, we forget to honor what we already hold. Gratitude is not a reaction, it's a perspective. A chosen lens through which life becomes fuller, even when it's flawed.

> **Gratitude turns what we have into enough. — Aesop**

We often measure our lives against others, their success, their happiness, their possessions. But comparison clouds blessings. Gratitude clears the lens.

To be grateful is not to be in denial of difficulties. It's to acknowledge the whole picture and still choose to focus on the good. Not because the bad isn't real, but because the good is just as real and yet often overlooked.

Gratitude invites calm. It shifts our energy from restlessness to recognition. It reminds us that abundance isn't always about having more, but about seeing more in what you have.

Practice helps. Start with three things each morning. A kind gesture. A withdrawal. A breath. Gratitude grows when it's named.

In relationships, gratitude softens edges. In hardship, it lends hope. In everyday moments, it creates magic.

It's a blessing we all carry, often quietly. But when expressed, it becomes a blessing shared.

Years ago, I tried a gratitude journal for the first time.

> **Enjoy the little things, for one day you may look back and realize they were the big things. — Robert Brault**

· WHAT LIFE TAUGHT ME ·

I was skeptical. But something shifted when I started noticing small things, the way morning light fell across my desk, the perfect crispness of a fresh apple. Gratitude made the ordinary feel like a gift.

Gratitude isn't an emotion, it's a perspective. It doesn't wait for perfect conditions. It reframes whatever is present.

We think of blessings as luck, but most of them are awareness. We don't need more to feel grateful. We need to see better.

· LET THIS SETTLE WITHIN YOU ·

What are three small things that brought you quiet joy this week? Did you notice them in the moment?

· TRY THIS IN YOUR OWN LIFE ·

Each day for the next 21 days, write down three specific things you're grateful for. Try not to repeat items. Let this simple act shift your focus from lack to abundance.

· LIFE ECHO: *INTEGRATE* ·

Gratitude isn't just a feeling. Make it a habit and it will reshape how you experience everything.

“ **He is a wise man who does not grieve for the things which he has not, but rejoices for those which he has. – Epictetus** ”

PART II

Mastering The Mind And Emotions

Cultivating peace, purpose, and presence.

In this section, we explore the delicate balance between inner desire and outer action. These chapters focus on emotional clarity, patient timing, sustainable joy, and the wisdom of restraint. As the LIFE Method continues, readers are encouraged to shape their internal world, not by force, but through awareness, boundaries, and self-compassion.

6. Wait For The Right Time

7. The Strategy To Be Happy

8. Don’t Let Aspirations Consume You

9. Conserve Yourself

10. Let Go To Move Forward

6

CHAPTER 6

Wait For The Right Time

CHAPTER 6: WAIT FOR THE RIGHT TIME

We live in a world that glorifies urgency. Everything is expected fast; techniques, results, success, answers. But life isn't a race; it's a rhythm! Sometimes, the wisest thing we can do is, to wait.

Waiting doesn't mean being inactive. It means being **intentional** with your energy. It means looking for the right moment to act, rather than forcing every door open.

In our culture of hustle, people run after time as though it's slipping away. But what if, instead, we learn to flow

> **Nature doesn't rush, yet everything is accomplished. — Lao Tzu**

with it?

There's a beauty in patience that often goes unnoticed. It tests and refines our virtues like faith, courage, restraint. It teaches us that **not everything blooms at once.**

> **Keep a quiet heart, sit like a tortoise, walk fast like a pigeon, and sleep like a dog. — Indian proverb**

When life puts you on pause, don't panic. Use the stillness. Reflect, Observe, Realign. These quiet stretches are often where our next version begins to form.

Impatience can cost us more than we know. Words spoken too soon, decisions rushed in fear, relationships abandoned before their season; all of them can be the consequences of moving ahead of life's timing.

Even curiosity, when turned obsessive, consumes the wonder it once held. We end up filling every silence with noise, every space with movement. But **wisdom needs room to breathe.**

So pause!

Wait before reacting.

Wait before quitting.

Wait before judging.

Wait before speaking.

This isn't inaction, it's mindfulness.

Because the right time will always feel less like pressure... and more like peace.

• WHAT LIFE TAUGHT ME •

Once, in a rush to make something happen, I pushed ahead too early; a job I wasn't ready for, a conversation that needed more time.

The result? Strain. Regret.

We often underestimate the wisdom of waiting.

Life has seasons. Sometimes the best action is inaction. Patience isn't inertness, it's precision.

Waiting gives you the gift of preparation and perspective. And while retrospect, the things that felt delayed are often arriving just on schedule.

• LET THIS SETTLE WITHIN YOU •

What area of your life might benefit from stillness instead of action right now?

• LIFE ECHO: *FLOW* •

Timing matters. Trusting life's pace brings ease instead of friction.

“ Cool your heels before you take the leap. — Swati Joshi ”

7

CHAPTER 7

The Strategy To Be Happy

CHAPTER 7: THE STRATEGY TO BE HAPPY

Happiness isn't a destination. It's not hidden in the future or buried in a treasure chest waiting to be found. It's a strategy. It's a way of seeing, choosing, and living.

We often treat happiness like a bonus just as something we get after achieving, solving, or proving. But if happiness is always on the other side of a goal, we never truly arrive.

The truth is, happiness isn't found. It's practiced.

> **Most folks are as happy as they make up their minds to be. — Abraham Lincoln**

A strategy doesn't mean faking joy or ignoring problems. It means creating small, sustainable habits that lead you back to contentment again and again. Gratitude, presence, purpose, compassion; all of these are not one-time feelings, they are muscles to be trained.

Your strategy might begin with what you consume. It's not just about food, but news, conversations, and thoughts. It may include movement, sleep, journaling, prayer, or time spent with nature.

The key is, make happiness **intentional**.

> **"Happiness is not something ready made. It comes from your own actions. — Dalai Lama"**

You can't wait for perfect days. You build better days, one mindful choice at a time. Talk gently to yourself. Forgive often. Laugh easily. Stay curious. Be kind to strangers. Leave room for wonder.

There will be hard seasons. Happiness doesn't erase them, but it surely does soften them.

A good strategy doesn't chase happiness.

It invites it.

It nurtures it.

It stays ready for it.

And over the time, that translates into a life well lived.

• WHAT LIFE TAUGHT ME •

Happiness isn't a grand prize. It's a decision, made daily. I once spent months chasing milestones that I thought would bring joy, then I realized that unscripted moments like a masala tea with a friend, a long walk with husband every weekend, or giving roti to the cow that visits me everyday were also the best one leading me to bliss.

We need a personal happiness strategy. Not a list of achievements, but rituals of meaning.

Design your life to include,

- Small joys
- Gentle boundaries
- Time with people who light you up
- Moments to breathe

• LET THIS SETTLE WITHIN YOU •

What five things (big or small) consistently lift your mood? Are they part of your routine?

• TRY THIS IN YOUR OWN LIFE •

Create a two-column list. In the left column, write

things that energize you. In the right, things that deplete you. Start scheduling your day around the left column.

· LIFE ECHO: *INTEGRATE* ·

Turn happiness into a habit, not a finish line.

> **Start sifting significant from trivial and there will be more room for peace and happiness. — Swati Joshi**

8

CHAPTER 8

Don't Let Aspirations Consume You

CHAPTER 8: DON'T LET ASPIRATIONS CONSUME YOU

Aspiration is beautiful. It pulls us towards growth, ambition, and new possibilities. But unchecked, it can become a silent thief, that may be robbing us of the joy of now.

We live in a world of milestones; next degree, next job, next house, next level. And while striving can be noble, it can also be exhausting when it leaves no space to savor life as it is.

What begins as motivation can morph into obsession.

You can do anything, but not everything.—David Allen

We start bidding our worth to our output, our peace to our performance, our happiness to our hustle.

The problem isn't in dreaming big. It's in forgetting that rest, contentment, and simplicity are also worthy goals.

Ambition is only noble when it does not devour the soul. — Francis Bacon

Sometimes, the most courageous act is to pause. To say, "I am enough for today." Not because you've stopped growing, but because you've started respecting your limits.

Remember, life isn't a checklist. It's not about constant upgrades. It's about rhythm. And peace is found not in acceleration, but in alignment.

Aspire to grow, but need not to burn out trying to bloom.

Aspire to evolve, but don't forget to enjoy who you are becoming.

The future is yours to shape. Just don't lose yourself building it.

· WHAT LIFE TAUGHT ME ·

There was a time when I said yes to every opportunity. Ambition disguised itself as productivity, and I wore exhaustion like a badge. But in chasing more, I began to lose what mattered the most.

Aspirations are wonderful until they own you.

Success shouldn't come at the cost of presence, health, or joy. Choose goals that align, not overwhelm.

I understand that many of you might not agree, but just try calculating the cost you're going to pay. If your inner voice approves the loss, you can continue chasing your dreams without slowing down.

• LET THIS SETTLE WITHIN YOU •

What's one ambition you're chasing that might need redefining or releasing?

• LIFE ECHO: *FLOW* •

Let go of what doesn't align. The right aspirations will energize, not exhaust you.

“ **Don’t let the star you follow become the chain that drags you. — Swati Joshi** ”

9

CHAPTER 9

Conserve Yourself

CHAPTER 9: CONSERVE YOURSELF

We often pour ourselves into everything, like in work, family, commitments etc. until we're running on fumes. But true strength isn't about relentless giving. It's about knowing when to pause, protect, and replenish your energy.

You are not a limitless resource.

You are not a machine.

Every living thing in nature follows a rhythm of use and rest. Trees shed. Rivers slow. Even the Earth turns her face from the Sun for half a day! ;) Why should we expect ourselves to operate without reprieve?

You don't have to set yourself on fire to keep others warm. — Penny Reid

We're taught to admire selflessness. But unchecked, it turns into depletion. And burnout doesn't just affect your productivity, but also reshapes your personality. It steals your spark.

> **Rest is not idleness, and to lie sometimes on the grass... is by no means a waste of time. — John Lubbock**

To conserve yourself means,

- Saying no without guilt.
- Setting boundaries that protect your peace.
- Listening to your body before it shouts.
- Taking breaks before you break.

Self-care isn't selfish. It's responsible.

You cannot serve well, love deeply, or create meaningfully from an empty vessel.

So rest!! It's not just any reward, but a right.

'A well deserved break or vacay' is just a showoff!

Because all of us have the right

- To protect our joy.
- To preserve our energy.

It's because what you sustain within, you can then maintain for others.

• WHAT LIFE TAUGHT ME •

We talk about time management, but what about energy management? I used to think burning out was normal. That you give your best by giving your all. But depletion is not a virtue.

You are a finite resource. Protect your mornings. Guard your peace. Say no with love.

The most generous people I know are not the busiest. They are the ones who preserve themselves well enough to give meaningfully.

• LET THIS SETTLE WITHIN YOU •

Where are you spending energy that doesn't replenish you? What boundary could help?

• LIFE ECHO: *LISTEN* •

Your body and mood are always speaking. Tune in before you hit empty.

"Selflessness when unchecked, turns into depletion. — Swati Joshi"

10

CHAPTER 10

Let Go To Move Forward

CHAPTER 10: LET GO TO MOVE FORWARD

We carry the baggage of old regrets, painful memories, outdated dreams more than we need. We simply cling to them because they once mattered. But sometimes, what once served us now weighs us down.

Letting go doesn't mean forgetting. It means freeing up the space needed for what's next.

When we hold too tightly to 'what it was', we miss a chance to grab 'what it could be'. Just like a clenched fist can't hold something new, **a heart full of 'Yesterday' has little room for 'Tomorrow'**.

We're never taught that letting go is not passive. It's

> **Some of us think holding on makes us strong, but sometimes it is letting go. — Hermann Hesse**

a courageous act. It means choosing healing over resentment, peace over perfection, and growth over comfort.

We should let go,

- Of relationships that no longer bring life.
- Of identities that no longer fit.
- Of outcomes we cannot control.
- Of the need to always be right, liked, or ahead.

In this process, something unexpected happens. We regain lightness. We remember who we are underneath all the armor.

> **You can't start the next chapter if you keep rereading the last one. — Michael McMillian**

Letting go isn't giving up. It's giving in to life, to change, to your own becoming.

Move forward, not because the past is erased, but because the future deserves your full presence.

Some of the most important steps you'll take will begin with what you leave behind.

I used to enjoy myself being a multitasker, stretching my limits in crushing every episode, every challenge a new day was bringing. Until one day, I read the same paragraph three times, replied to an email I didn't remember, and started missing moments with loved ones.

It was a nudge!

Multitasking isn't a badge. It's often a barrier to presence.

• LET THIS SETTLE WITHIN YOU •

When was the last time you were fully present? What did it feel like?

• LIFE ECHO: *INTEGRATE* •

Presence is the root of quality, in work, love, and life.

> **Letting go the unwanted, undesirable or unpleasant is the easiest way to overcome the feeling that makes you sick. — Swati Joshi**

PART III

Social And Emotional Wealth

Building bonds that nourish and sustain us.

This section invites readers to rediscover the joy, healing, and strength that emerge through human connections. From playfulness and laughter to trust and kindness, these chapters reveal how relationships form the emotional architecture of a fulfilling life. The LIFE Method here blossoms outward, extending empathy, love, and meaning into our shared world.

11

CHAPTER 11

Merriment Is The Way

CHAPTER 11: MERRIMENT IS THE WAY

Living isn't just about survival, it's about joy. Yet somewhere along the way, we start believing that happiness has to be earned through struggle, achievement, or accumulation.

But what if merriment is not a luxury but a need?

We all carry stress. Across generations, this hasn't changed. But the way we release it has. Today, many forget how to have lighthearted fun. Playing a game, laughing with friends, or singing out of tune are dismissed as "Childish". But these acts are profoundly human!

We don't stop playing because we grow old; we grow old because we stop playing. — George Bernard Shaw

Fun isn't trivial. It resets your nervous system. It balances your chemistry. It reminds you that you're alive, not just functioning.

We often chase happiness as a destination. But merriment teaches us that it's a moment. One that doesn't need perfect conditions. It just needs permission.

> **The most wasted of all days is one without laughter. — E. E. Cummings**

You don't have to join a club or buy tickets. Play with your kids unconcerned of rules, share jokes with your neighbors, sing loudly while cooking, dance in your room when no one's watching. These aren't distractions from life, they are life.

In a world full of striving, lightness is a revolt. It reconnects us. It heals relationships. It builds bridges across age, culture, and pain.

Even a child forgets pain when play begins. And we also can do the same very often.

So make time for laughter.

Make time to be silly.

Make time for joy.

Because merriment isn't the opposite of seriousness. It's the companion of wisdom.

And it might just be your secret to a longer, happier life.

• WHAT LIFE TAUGHT ME •

I once watched a group of elderly women in a park laughing uncontrollably over something small. Their joy was infectious, and for a moment, I forgot all the hardships of life. It reminded me that merriment isn't futile. It's essential.

Joy is not the result of everything going right. It's the art of being fully alive in the moment.

Merriment keeps the soul light. It's not distraction; it's resilience wrapped in play.

• LET THIS SETTLE WITHIN YOU •

When was the last time you laughed without restraint? What made that moment possible?

• LIFE ECHO: *FLOW* •

Let laughter flow without needing a big reason. It rebalances the soul.

> “Mirth is an art of being fully alive in the moment. — Swati Joshi”

12

CHAPTER 12

Connect (Invisible Threads)

CHAPTER 12: CONNECT INVISIBLE THREADS

We often underestimate the power of connection. Yet, study after study shows that relationships are not just nice to have, they're vital for a long, meaningful life.

Being socially connected improves our immune system, lifts our mood, and can even extend our lifespan by up to 50%. That's not just poetic, it's proven.

But in today's world, solitude is often romanticized. While alone time has its benefits, isolation is an entirely different condition. Over the time, it quietly chips away

The most basic and powerful way to connect to another person is to listen. Just listen. — Rachel Naomi Remen

at our mental, emotional, and even physical health.

Midlife is especially vulnerable to this. We're balancing families, careers, aging parents, and future plans. Ironically, in the effort to give our loved ones everything, we often lose the people themselves. Or worse, we start losing ourselves.

> **People need people. Whether we admit it or not. — Benjamin Zephaniah**

Look around. When was the last time you had a truly heartfelt conversation, offline?

Connection is about presence, not performance. It's not measured by likes, followers, or digital reach. It's felt in a shared laugh, a knowing silence, a cup of tea passed across the table.

It's also true that not all connections are comforting. Some teach us hard lessons. Some test our patience. But if we stay open, reflective, and willing to grow, even those bleak interactions contribute to our emotional resilience.

It's not the number of friends that counts, but the quality of those bonds definitely do.

Trusting people again, even after being hurt takes enormous courage. In the same way, reaching out, listening without judging, and choosing forgiveness when ego demands revenge take the same amount of audacity.

Science agrees with ancient wisdom that being seen, heard, and valued is essential to our wellbeing.

So connect!

Stay in touch.

Invite people in.

Because a shared life is not just happier.

It's healthier.

And those invisible threads?

They might just be holding us all together.

• WHAT LIFE TAUGHT ME •

I remember receiving a call from a childhood friend after years apart. The words flowed buoyantly, the warmth was extending to our hearts. Some threads never break.

We humans are wired for connection, eye contact, shared silence, honest conversation, not for likes or follows.

In a fragmented world, connection is sacred.

• LET THIS SETTLE WITHIN YOU •

Who are three people you feel deeply connected to? What makes those connections matter?

• TRY THIS IN YOUR OWN LIFE •

Each day this week, message one person with a genuine check-in.

No agenda.

Just presence.

• LIFE ECHO: *LISTEN* •

Connection begins by listening, even between the lines.

> **“We all are hues of a masterpiece called life; be someone’s missing color and let them add a few to your canvas. — Swati Joshi”**

13

CHAPTER 13

Earn The Honor Of Living

CHAPTER 13: EARN THE HONOR OF LIVING

In the daily rhythm of life, it's easy to forget how precious simply being alive is. We grow used to our routines, our comforts, even our complaints. But beneath it all, life remains a gift, one we did not earn, but one we can honor.

To live well is not to chase perfection. It is to walk with purpose, with integrity, and with care for others.

> **Life is a gift. And it offers us the privilege, opportunity, and responsibility to give something back. — Tony Robbins**

There's a quiet dignity in doing your best when no one is watching, in showing up with honesty, in lifting others without needing applause.

You make a living by what you get. You make a life by what you give. — Winston Churchill

Earning the honor of living means

- Keeping your word.
- Making space for others to grow.
- Speaking truth, even when it's inconvenient.
- Choosing kindness when anger is easier.

It means becoming someone your younger self would be proud of and your older self would express gratitude for.

I'm not talking about being extraordinary. It's about being accountable for the ordinary.

Because how you live shapes not only your legacy, but your own sense of worth.

I must remind you that you don't misconstrue Self esteem for Self worth.

Honor of living as a human being gives you the belief

that you are "good enough" simply because you exist. It translates how you carry yourself within the grander tapestry of existence.

Live with honor.

Give more than you take.

And let your life be a thank you note to existence itself.

• WHAT LIFE TAUGHT ME •

There is a difference between merely existing and truly living. And living well is an honor earned not by perfection, but by presence, kindness, courage.

We earn this honor not in grand gestures, but in daily choices; standing up for someone, admitting a mistake, forgiving without being asked.

• LET THIS SETTLE WITHIN YOU •

What are three ways you've honored life this past month, however smaller?

• LIFE ECHO: *EVOLVE* •

Growth is not just in what you gather, but also in how you give.

“Values, intentions and actions aligned together make a strong foundation for a meaningful life. — Swati Joshi”

14

CHAPTER 14

Allow Yourself To Be Cheated (Trust Again)

CHAPTER 14: ALLOW YOURSELF TO BE CHEATED (TRUST AGAIN)

There is an ancient wisdom in the phrase "allow yourself to be cheated." It does not advocate naïveté or weakness. It speaks to a mindset that chooses grace over guardedness, and openness over suspicion.

To live a life of interdependence, you can occasionally risk being hurt. Not because you enjoy pain, but because you believe that trust is a more powerful foundation than fear.

> **The best way to find out if you can trust somebody is to trust them. — Ernest Hemingway**

When we wall ourselves in with skepticism, it might act as some defense mechanism, but we also lock out joy, companionship, and renewal. In doing so we don't just filter out the bad; we create a barrier that prevents the good from entering as well.

Yes, people will disappoint you. Some will take more than they give. But don't let that convince you to become someone who never opens the door again.

Trust wisely, but trust nonetheless.

To love at all is to be vulnerable. — C.S. Lewis

To allow yourself to be cheated is

- To Accept that not all kindness will be returned
- To Offer the benefit of doubt without keeping score
- To Choose to believe **rationally** in someone's better self

This isn't weakness. It's **spiritual courage.**

Because a heart that dares to trust again, even after being bruised, is a heart that refuses to be conquered by fear.

In this radical vulnerability lies your greatest strength!

• WHAT LIFE TAUGHT ME •

I once trusted someone who betrayed me deeply. It took years to let that go. But I learned this — mistrust builds walls, and trust, even though broken, builds bridges.

To trust means choosing possibility over protection.

Yes, you might get hurt. But you might also be healed. Just don't let the same experiences make a repetitive pattern in your life.

Trusting people is inevitable for a quality life, just learn to draw that thin line between bravery and stupidity.

• LET THIS SETTLE WITHIN YOU •

Who have you been guarding your heart from? What would it mean to trust them, even a little?

• LIFE ECHO: *INTEGRATE* •

Trust is not a leap, it's a series of steps toward connection.

“

A bruised heart that chooses to trust again is the bravest. — Swati Joshi

”

15

CHAPTER 15

Healing Through Others

CHAPTER 15: HEALING THROUGH OTHERS

Healing is often seen as a solitary journey. But in reality, much of our restoration happens in the presence of others. Through conversation. Through shared silence. Through the simple but profound experience of being witnessed.

"Hiding away" is the natural instinct when we are hurt.

When we're in pain, isolation feels like a shield that often ends up turning into a cage. When we are alone, our internal monologue can become a vacuum of self-criticism or distorted reality.

Just like pain, shame also breeds in secret. Disgrace

> **We don't heal in isolation, but in community. — S. Kelley Harrell**

intimidates that if people would know the real you or what you've been through, they'd leave.

Connection is the ultimate antidote to the feeling of being crumbled.

Whether it's a friend, family member or anyone you feel safe with, listens without judgment, holds space without fixing, and accepts you without condition, healing begins.

We heal when we see ourselves reflected in another's story.

We heal when someone comprehend our pain without needing to explain it away.

We heal when we are reminded that our scars do not disqualify us from belonging.

To heal through others,

People start to heal the moment they feel heard. – Cheryl Richardson

- Let yourself be seen, even in your mess.
- Reach out when silence gets heavy.
- Offer empathy, not advice.
- Be the kind of presence you once needed.

We are all both wounded and wise. And it is in this beautiful contradiction that we find the power to mend one another.

Healing is not always loud. Sometimes, it's a quiet moment of connection that says, "Me too.. I understand because I've been there once."

And in that moment, something shifts.

A little more light comes in.

And the journey becomes bearable, a bit easier, together.

• WHAT LIFE TAUGHT ME •

There is no healing in isolation. The deepest wounds I had, were cured not by solitude, but by shared experience, by someone simply saying, "Me too… I understand!"

People heal people. Stories save us. Presence repairs.

Don't underestimate the quiet healing that happens through a hug, a shared laugh, a moment of mutual recognition.

• LET THIS SETTLE WITHIN YOU •

Who helped you heal something you thought was incurable? How?

• LIFE ECHO: *LISTEN + EVOLVE* •

Healing is a loop, the more we receive, the more we're able to give.

It takes two to damage, and two to mend. — Swati Joshi

PART IV

The Soulful Life

Living wisely, dying empty, and leaving gently.

In this final section, the LIFE Method comes full circle, able to encourage readers to embrace impermanence, legacy, and meaning. These chapters explore purpose, mortality, and the grace of letting go. Here, we are asked not only to live well, but to leave well that's with clarity, contribution, and peace.

16

CHAPTER 16

Why Are We Really Here?

CHAPTER 16: WHY ARE WE REALLY HERE?

This question, 'why are we really here?' echoes in quiet moments. It visits us in heartbreak, in awe, in stillness. It halts behind our daily routines, gently asking us to look beyond the scope.

We are not here just to consume, to accumulate, or to chase fleeting highs. We are here to receive, to contribute, to grow, to love. to witness beauty and suffering, and to respond with something that makes sense.

It's a massive relief to realize that purpose of life doesn't

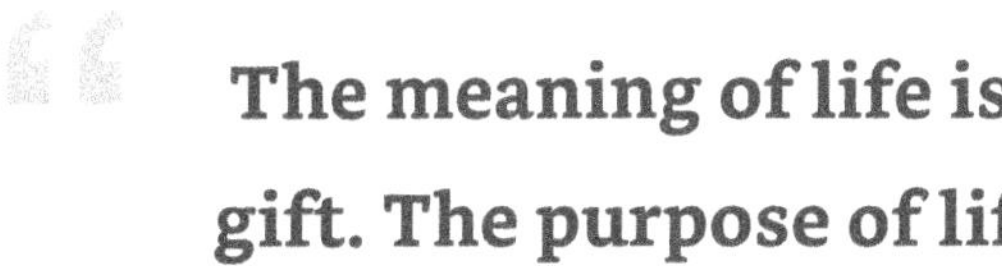

> **The meaning of life is to find your gift. The purpose of life is to give it away. — Pablo Picasso**

have to be grand. It can be quiet. Purpose needs not to be a project or a performance, it should be about practice.

Practice as in when you are stuck in traffic or at a function or with people you aren't fond of, you can practice being a patient person. The purpose is always there; it must becomes a tool you use rather than a prize you chase.

It can reflect in nursing a garden, raising a child, showing up consistently for a friend, or doing work that supports you.

> **The purpose of life is not to be happy. It is to be useful, to be honorable, to be compassionate. — Ralph Waldo Emerson**

You are here

- To experience and evolve
- To give what only you can
- To turn your pain into wisdom
- To live a life that reflects your deepest truths

When we align with purpose, we live more fully. We feel less lost and more rooted. And we begin to measure our days not by what we've gained, but by what we can give.

Purpose is all about the clarity that you don't have all the answers, but you can keep asking the question.

Because the question itself leads you to the life only you can live.

• WHAT LIFE TAUGHT ME •

There were times when everyone and everything around felt pointless. Work felt like routine, conversations felt rehearsed. People seemed fake. Then a single question changed everything, "What am I truly here for?"

Purpose isn't a one-time discovery. It's a thread you follow, a lens you adjust.

Sometimes, it's bold.

Sometimes, it's hushed.

To ask "why" isn't permissive.

It's gallant.

• LET THIS SETTLE WITHIN YOU •

When do you feel most aligned with your purpose? What are you doing in those moments?

• LIFE ECHO: *LISTEN* •

You already know more than you think. The answers often echo from within.

“We are here to transform solitude into belonging through giving, receiving, witnessing and helping.
— Swati Joshi”

17

CHAPTER 17

Build A Life Worth Remembering

CHAPTER 17: BUILD A LIFE WORTH REMEMBERING

We often worry about how we will be remembered. But legacy is not built in big declarations.

Legacy is often sold as a monument we build at the end of our lives, but in reality, it is the residue we leave behind in every room we walk through.

It's shaped by daily decisions, in how we treat people, the promises we keep, and the love and compassion we

> **Carve your name on hearts, not tombstones. A legacy is etched into the minds of others and the stories they share about you. — Shannon L. Alder**

share.

To build a life worth remembering, don't chase reminiscence. Chase meaning.

The world won't remember the exact numbers in your bank account or the size of your home. But it will remember the way you showed up for others. The way you smiled at strangers. The way you made people feel seen.

> **Your legacy is every life you've touched. — Maya Angelou**

Your presence or absence won't echo in any accumulation, it will reflect in the eyes and hearts of the people whose life you've changed. No grand or extravagant gestures are required, a couple of kind words can also do.

Start small —

- Leave a kind word where silence used to live.
- Teach what you've learned.
- Stand up for someone else.

Legacy isn't something we leave behind; it's something we live into.

Live today as if it will echo. Because trust me, it will.

And let your life be a story worth retelling.

Legacy isn't about being known by many. It's about being remembered deeply by a few.

• WHAT LIFE TAUGHT ME •

A neighbor of mine passed away quietly. No fanfare. But at his memorial, person after person stood up with stories of his quiet kindness. He built a meaningful life without seeking attention.

Build yours not just with success, but with substance.

• LET THIS SETTLE WITHIN YOU •

What values do you want to be remembered for?

Are they present in your daily life?

• LIFE ECHO: *EVOLVE* •

Legacy is built one small, consistent act at a time.

“Let your values coincide with your actions, and people will keep you in their hearts like a priceless souvenir. — Swati Joshi”

18

CHAPTER 18

Living Light (Letting Go)

CHAPTER 18: LIVING LIGHT (LETTING GO)

We carry so much; Grudges, Expectations, Guilt, Stuff. And somewhere along the way, all this weight begins to dull our joy.

> **The things you own end up owning you. — Chuck Palahniuk**

To live light is not to live less. It is to live free.

Letting go is not giving up. It's giving space for newness, for clarity, for peace.

It means

- Setting free relationships that deplete you.
- Cast off perfectionism.

- Forgiving what's behind you.
- Simplifying what surrounds you.

We often fear letting go because we confuse it with loss. But more often, it is a path to gain.

If you are clenching your fist tightly around a handful of your past experiences, a resentment, a betrayal, a failed idea; your hand is occupied. You can't use it to pick up anything new, rather vital.

Letting go is simply opening the fist for

- More presence.
- More room to breathe.
- More alignment with what truly matters.

“

You only lose what you cling to. — Buddha

Declutter your mind. Unburden your soul. Loosen your grip on restraint.

And you will find that lightness is not emptiness.

It's clarity.

It's strength.

It's the sound of your spirit exhaling.

• WHAT LIFE TAUGHT ME •

I used to hold on to everything, people, old stories, occurrences. I believed that to keep meant to care. But over the time, I learned that 'to let go' doesn't mean 'to lose'. It's a gift to your future self.

To live light is to live free.

Release what no longer serves. Make room for what's next.

• LET THIS SETTLE WITHIN YOU •

What are you holding onto that is weighing you down? What might happen if you release it?

• LIFE ECHO: *FLOW* •

Letting go is not a failure. It's faith in new beginnings.

“ Declutter, Cleanse and Move on, is the exact order of letting go! — Swati Joshi ”

19

CHAPTER 19

Leave Goodness Behind

CHAPTER 19: LEAVE GOODNESS BEHIND

At the end of a life, what remains? Not titles. Not possessions. But the goodness we planted in others because it is not a destination, but a chain reaction. Sometimes, your single act of kindness is powerful enough to alter the trajectory of someone else's life.

To leave goodness behind is to live with intention, not just ambition. It means your impact is measured in memories.

We underestimate the power of small good deeds. We usually don't estimate how a listening ear, a shared

> **What you leave behind is not what is engraved in stone monuments, but what is woven into the lives of others. — Pericles**

meal, a moment of honesty can do wonders. These become seeds that grow and bear fruits long after we're gone.

> **I want to leave this world a little better for me having been here. — Jim Henson**

To leave goodness behind

- Share your wisdom freely.
- Lift others without needing credit.
- Apologize when needed. Forgive even when it's hard.
- Choose compassion over convenience.

Goodness is not loud. It doesn't clamor for recognition. But it lingers like aroma. Kindness, meekness, benevolence, integrity, goodwill whatever you name it, has an aura. It heals. It inspires.

And long after your name fades from memory, the kindness you showed will continue to echo.

Let that be your legacy.

We spend so much energy chasing more. But what if we measured life by how much goodness we leave behind?

Leave trails of kindness. Leave hope in conversations. Let people feel lighter after knowing you.

• LET THIS SETTLE WITHIN YOU •

What kind of goodness do you want to leave behind, starting today?

• LIFE ECHO: *INTEGRATE* •

Make goodness a pattern, not a performance.

“ You need not to showcase goodness; it reaches them like a fragrance in the air. — Swati Joshi ”

20

CHAPTER 20

Long Live Life (Final Reflection)

CHAPTER 20: LONG LIVE LIFE (FINAL REFLECTION)

In the end, what matters is not how long we live, but how deeply we did. Life is not measured only in years, but in presence, in meaning, in courage.

'Long live life!' is not just a wish; it is a call to action.

Living long is an endurance sport that requires daily training. It is the realization that while we cannot control the length of the string, we can certainly control the strength of the weave.

The action here is lifelong learning. To live long is to remain curious, preventing the stagnation that often accompanies aging.

> **Tell me, what is it you plan to do with your one wild and precious life? — Mary Oliver**

It's a reminder to

- Speak truth with kindness.
- Chase wonder instead of comfort.
- Rest without guilt.
- Give love without condition.

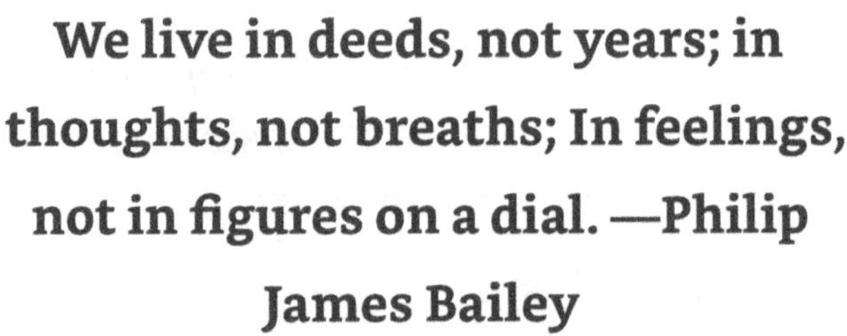

We live in deeds, not years; in thoughts, not breaths; In feelings, not in figures on a dial. —Philip James Bailey

This book is not any instruction manual. It's a mirror. And possibly, a nudge.

You already know most of what's written here. It's nothing more than you knowing the life in your quiet moments, your inner voice, your small decisions.

True living is found in self-awareness. It's the act of listening to your intuition and realizing that your life is built, brick by brick, through your most silent moments and smallest still significant actions.

So return to them. Trust them. Live them.

Because when we do, we aren't just adding more years, we're expanding our lives.

Long live curiosity.

Long live kindness.

Long live courage.

Long live life.

And may you live it well.

This book began as a collection of reflections and became a quiet manifesto for living meaningfully.

· WHAT LIFE TAUGHT ME ·

To live well is not to have all the answers, but to ask better questions.

To slow down. To notice. To love. To listen. To evolve.

Long live life, not because it's always easy, but because it's always worth it.

What is one lesson from this book you want to carry forward for the rest of your life?

· LET THIS SETTLE WITHIN YOU ·

A meaningful life isn't static.

Keep growing.

· LIFE ECHO: *EVOLVE* ·

Keep giving.

Keep going.

"Nurture the good in yourself, become better for all, and leave the best for the rest. — Swati Joshi"

Letter to the Reader

Dear Reader,

If you've arrived here, page after page, quietly listening and reflecting, then I want to thank you not just for reading this book, but for honoring your own stillness in a world that's forgetting to make room for it.

These chapters aren't meant to shout. They are written anticipating that they might accompany you like an old friend with warmth, understanding n composure.

I don't have all the answers. No one can ever have, I believe. But I've lived enough moments, questions, and quiet observations and get to know this truth about life, as Richard Todd Canton mentions **'life never asks us to be perfect, it needs us to be present.'** Be there to notice the small wisdom in everyday things. Be there to choose gentleness even when it's hard. Be there to believe that living well isn't about grand gestures, but the honest ones.

I wish that something in these pages nudged your

thinking or softened your pace even just a little.

And if, one fine day, you find yourself returning to one of these pages, not for any advice but just for comfort, I will consider that the highest honor.

May you live gently.

May you listen deeply.

And may your days, even the quiet ones, feel fully yours.

With love, warmth and gratitude,

Swati

www.ingramcontent.com/pod-product-compliance
Lightning Source LLC
Chambersburg PA
CBHW021215280126
38842CB00024B/222

* 9 7 8 9 3 5 6 5 5 4 2 4 5 *